Letter Name, Volume 2

Words
Their Way
CLASSROOM

SAVVAS
LEARNING COMPANY

Cover Antagain/E+/Getty Images; ARTIKAL/Shutterstock; CVR: owatta/Shutterstock; whitemomo/Shutterstock

1 (Hot) Simone van den Berg/Alamy Stock Photo; 3 (Hot) Simone van den Berg/Alamy Stock Photo; 5 (Can) Thinkstock/Getty Images, (Pin) Ablestock/Photos to Go/Getty Images; 7 (Can) Thinkstock/Getty Images, (Pin) Ablestock/Photos to Go/Getty Images; 9 (Crab) Getty Images, 11 (Crab) Getty Images; 13 (Mop) Stockbyte/Thinkstock/Getty Images, (Puppy) Corbis; 15 (Mop) Stockbyte/Thinkstock/Getty Images, (Puppy) Corbis; 17 (Bug) Brand X Pictures/Thinkstock/Getty Images, (Pig) Anat-oli/Shutterstock; 19 (Bug) Brand X Pictures/Thinkstock/Getty Images, (Pig) Anat-oli/Shutterstock; 21 (Bell) Getty Images, (Pill) Catshila/Shutterstock; 23 (Bell) Jupiter Images/Getty Images, (Pill) Catshila/Shutterstock; 25 (Chick) Getty Images, (Duck) Shutterstock; 27 (Chick) Getty Images, (Duck) Shutterstock; 29 (Cash) Thinkstock/Getty Images, (Fish) Eric Isselée/Shutterstock; 31 (Cash) Thinkstock/Getty Images, (Fish) Eric Isselée/Shutterstock; 41,44,45,47,48,53,55,56,57,59 (Pig) Anat-oli/Shutterstock; 105 (Bat) Getty Images, (Cash) Thinkstock/Getty Images, (Duck) Shutterstock, (Mill) Photos to Go/Getty Images, (Pin) Ablestock/Photos to Go/Getty Images, (Pot) Margouillat Photo/Shutterstock;106 (Bell) Jupiter Images/Getty Images, (Can) Thinkstock/Getty Images, (Crab) Getty Images, (Eggs) Jupiter Images/Getty Images, (Fish) Eric Isselée/Shutterstock, (Fox) Jeremy Woodhouse/Getty Images, (Frog) Malcolm Schuyl/Shutterstock, (Pot) Margouillat Photo/Shutterstock; 107 (Drink) Goodshoot/Jupiter Images/Getty Images, (King) Thinkstock/Getty Images, (Skunk) Thinkstock/Getty Images, (Swing) Getty Images, (Tank) Shutterstock, (Tent) Shutterstock; 108 (Car) Adisa/Shutterstock, (Card) Aaron Amat/Shutterstock, (Cart) Andrey Armyagov/Shutterstock, (Corn) Jupiter Images/Getty Images, (Crab) Getty Images, (Horn) Shutterstock, (Shark) Prochasson Frederic/Shutterstock, (Thorn) Evgeni S./Shutterstock, (Yard) Photos to Go/Getty Images.

ISBN 13: 978-1-4284-4188-0
ISBN-10:   1-4284-4188-3

8 21

Contents

Sort 25 Mixed Vowel Word Families
-at, -ot, -it 1

Sort 26 Mixed Vowel Word Families
-an, -in, -en, -un 5

Sort 27 Mixed Vowel Word Families
-ad, -ed, -ab, -ob 9

Sort 28 Mixed Vowel Word Families
-ap, -ip, -op, -up 13

Sort 29 Mixed Vowel Word Families
-ag, -eg, -ig, -og, -ug 17

Sort 30 Mixed Vowel Word Families
ill, ell, all 21

Sort 31 Mixed Vowel Word Families
-ack, -ick, -ock, -uck 25

Sort 32 Mixed Vowel Word Families
-ash, -ish, -ush 29

Sort 33 Mixed Vowel Word Families
-ang, -ank, -ing, -ink 33

Sort 34 Short Vowels a, o 37

Sort 35 Short Vowels i, u 41

Sort 36 Short Vowels e, i, o, u 45

Sort 37 Short Vowels in CVC Words a, o 49

Sort 38 Short Vowels in CVC Words i, u 53

Sort 39 Short Vowels in CVC
Words e, i, o, u 57

Sort 40 Short a, e, i Words with
Beginning Digraphs 61

Sort 41 Short a, i Words with
Beginning Blends 65

Sort 42 Short e, o, u Words with
Beginning Blends 69

Sort 43 Short Vowel Words with
Final Blends 73

Sort 44 Short Vowel Words with
Final Digraphs 77

Sort 45 "Mysterious" n and m 81

Sort 46 Words that End in -ng, -mp 85

Sort 47 Words that End in -nt, -nk,
and -nd 89

Sort 48 Short o and or 93

Sort 49 Short a and ar 97

Sort 50 Contractions 101

Spell Check 4   Mixed Vowel
               Word Families......................105

Spell Check 5   Short Vowel Words.............106

Spell Check 6   Preconsonantal Nasals 107

Spell Check 7   r-Influenced Vowels............108

cat	hot	sit
not	fit	that
bat	cot	dot
got	fat	bit
hit	mat	slot
spot	kit	flat
rat	lit	trot
pit	chat	quit

cat	hot	sit

b	r	fl	m	th			tr	d	sl	c	sp			h	k	l	b	qu
				-at							**-ot**							**-it**

sun	ten 10	pin	can
skin	fan	bun	thin
win	pen	man	then
run	chin	ran	plan
pan	grin	fun	hen
than	men	fin	when

Sort 26: Mixed Vowel Word Families -an, -in, -en, -un ⑤

sun	ten 10	pin	can

Sort 26: Mixed Vowel Word Families -an, -in, -en, -un (7)

f m pl th r	-an

ch gr w f	-in

wh m th h	-en

r f b	-un

Mixed Vowel Word Families -ad, -ed, -ab, -ob

cob	crab	bed	sad
tab	mad	rob	red
had	mob	fed	blob
lab	sob	bad	led
glad	glob	shed	pad
cab	sled	grab	job

Sort 27: Mixed Vowel Word Families -ad, -ed, -ab, -ob   (9)

cob	crab	bed	sad

Sort 27: Mixed Vowel Word Families -ad, -ed, -ab, -ob   (11)

Use one of the letters or blends to make a word with -ad, -ed, -ab, or -ob. Write each word on a line.

m gl b h	
	-ad

sh r sl f	
	-ed

gr c l t	
	-ab

r s gl j	
	-ob

cap	zip	mop	pup
flip	cup	whip	snap
top	clap	hop	zap
chop	hip	crop	tap
pop	up	dip	lap
trip	drop	ship	trap

Sort 28: Mixed Vowel Word Families -ap, -ip, -op, -up ⑬

pup

mop

zip

cap

Sort 28: Mixed Vowel Word Families -ap, -ip, -op, -up (15)

Use one of the letters or blends to make a word with -ap, -ip, -op, or -up. Write each word on a line.

-ap				
sn	z	l	tr	

-ip			
d	h	tr	fl

-op				
t	h	p	dr

-up	
c	p

bug	dog	pig	leg	tag
rug	log	bag	hug	rag
wig	big	peg	fig	wag
drug	frog	flag	Meg	jog
hog	beg	snag	plug	slug
jig	mug	twig	fog	dig

Sort 29: Mixed Vowel Word Families -ag, -eg, -ig, -og, -ug (17)

bug						
dog						
pig						
leg						
tag						

Sort 29: Mixed Vowel Word Families -ag, -eg, -ig, -og, -ug (19)

Use one of the letters to make a word with -ag, -eg, -ig, -og, or -ug. Write each word on a line.

w b r	-ag
b p l	-eg
b f d	-ig
h f l	-og
r b h	-ug

Sort 29: Mixed Vowel Word Families -ag, -eg, -ig, -og, -ug

pill	bell	ball
fell	bill	hall
will	fall	mall
fill	call	chill
well	tall	shell
small	smell	spill
sell	hill	tell

pill	bell	ball

f	w	h	m	ch					-ill

f	t	s	w	sh					-ell

b	c	h	f	t					-all

Mixed Vowel Word Families -ack, -ick, -ock, -uck

duck	lock	chick	black
trick	stuck	pack	truck
thick	clock	back	tuck
sack	pluck	kick	rock
lick	flock	brick	luck
block	dock	tack	rack

Sort 31: Mixed Vowel Word Families -ack, -ick, -ock, -uck (25)

duck	lock	chick	black

Sort 31: Mixed Vowel Word Families -ack, -ick, -ock, -uck (27)

l k ch th	-ick
p r bl t	-ack
tr l st d	-uck
r l d cl	-ock

fish 	cash	brush
rush	dash	wish
flash	swish	crush
fish	mush	blush
crash	flush	smash
hush	rash	dish
trash	mash	plush

fish	cash	brush

Use one of the letters to make a word with -ish, -ash, or -ush.
Write each word on a line.

w d sw f	m r cr d sm	br r h m cr
-ish	-ash	-ush

-ink	-ing	-ank	-ang
sang	ring	sink	sank
think	link	gang	bring
drink	clang	rang	king
blank	hang	bank	prank
blink	thank	sing	sting

Sort 33: Mixed Vowel Word Families -ang, -ank, -ing, -ink (33)

-ink	-ing	-ank	-ang

Sort 33: Mixed Vowel Word Families -ang, -ank, -ing, -ink (35)

Use one of the letters to make a word with -ang, -ank, -ing, or -ink. Write each word on the line.

s h cl r	-ang
r b s th bl	-ank
s st k br	-ing
l s dr th	-ink

(36) Sort 33: Mixed Vowel Word Families -ang, -ank, -ing, -ink

Short Vowels a, o

cat	sock	oddball		
top	hop	had	wag	ran
ham	box	lot	was	for
mop	hot	mom	cab	bag
fox	got	map	sad	jam
job				

cat					sock					oddball				

Sort 34: Short Vowels a, o 39

Say each word in the box. Print each word under the key word that has the same short vowel sound.

sad	bag	fox	hop
mom	job	ran	lot
got	cab	jam	wag

cat

sock

Short Vowels i, u

pig	cup	oddball
zip	jug	will	rub	rip
big	tub	cut	run	fun
win	him	hum	nut	gum
did	put	six	bit	pin
but				

oddball

cup

pig

Say each word in the box. Print each word under the key word that has the same short vowel sound.

six	gum	pin	bit
hum	fun	tub	cut
did	zip	nut	will

pig

cup

bed	pig	sock	cup
wet	six	pop	not
pet	miss	his	mud
mix	yes	hid	hot
let	bus	cub	bug
sun	bell		

cup					

sock					

pig					

bed					

Sort 36: Short Vowels e, i, o, u (47)

Say each word in the box. Print each word under the key word that has the same short vowel sound.

hid	cub	hot	six
wet	sun	bell	pop
his	not	mud	den

bed	pig	sock	cup

ă 	ŏ	oddballs
box	dad	fox
got	ran	had
top	has	wag
hop	jam	mom
cab	mop	rob
saw	job	was

oddball					

ŏ					

ă					

Sort 37: Short Vowels in CVC Words ă, ŏ (51)

Say each word in the box. Print each word under the box that shows its short vowel sound.

had	box	mom	dad
job	top	cab	has
got	fox	ran	wag

ă

ŏ

Sort 37: Short Vowels in CVC Words ă, ŏ

ĭ	ŭ	oddball
big	but	did
fun	win	gum
him	zip	hum
jug	put	rip
rub	cut	six
nut	bit	tub

oddball					

ŭ

ĭ

Sort 38: Short Vowels in CVC Words ĭ, ŭ (55)

Say each word in the box. Print each word under the box that shows its short vowel sound.

fun	win	gum	him
jug	cut	big	rub
rip	tub	bit	six

ĭ 🐷

ŭ ☕

Sort 38: Short Vowels in CVC Words ĭ, ŭ

Short Vowels in CVC Words ĕ, ĭ, ŏ, ŭ

Sort 39

oddball	ŭ	ŏ	ĭ	ĕ
hot	hid	get	cub	bus
mud	mix	let	boy	kit
her	his	pop	pet	not
		yes	tell	sip

Sort 39: Short Vowels in CVC Words ĕ, ĭ, ŏ, ŭ 57

oddball					

ŭ					

ŏ					

ĭ					

ĕ					

Sort 39: Short Vowels in CVC Words ĕ, ĭ, ŏ, ŭ   (59)

Say each word in the box. Print each word under the box that shows its short vowel sound.

bus	cub	yes	hid
hot	let	mix	mud
not	pet	pop	sip

ĕ

ĭ

ŏ

ŭ

Sort 39: Short Vowels in CVC Words ĕ, ĭ, ŏ, ŭ

that	chat	thick
them	than	chap
shed	then	thin
whip	shack	wham
chill	ship	chest
shell	check	when
chick	whiz	shall

Short a, e, i Words
With Beginning Digraphs

ă	ĕ	ĭ

Say each short vowel word. Print the word under the box that shows its short vowel sound.

them	than	chap	shed	then	thin
whip	shack	wham	chill	ship	chest
shell	check	that	chick	whiz	shall

ă	ĕ	ĭ

glad	clip	cram	drag	spin
slip	plan	grab	slid	skip
flag	flat	crab	trap	grill
ĭ	brag	grip	flip	brat
ă	drill	clap	drip	slap

Sort 41: Short a, i Words With Beginning Blends (65)

ĭ

ă

Say each word in the box. Print each word under the box that shows its short vowel sound.

glad	flip	slap	slip
brag	flag	clip	grill
drip	slid	flat	trap

ă

ĭ

Sort 41: Short a, i Words With Beginning Blends

ĕ	ŏ	ŭ
trot	club	sled
fret	plot	drop
bled	slug	plum
dress	cross	drum
plug	frog	drug
slob	truck	slot

Short e, o, u Words With Beginning Blends

ĕ	ŏ	ŭ

Sort 42: Short e, o, u Words With Beginning Blends (71)

Draw two pictures of things with the short vowel sounds of e, o, and u. Write the word below each picture.

ĕ	ŏ	ŭ

Sort 42: Short e, o, u Words With Beginning Blends

ŭ	ŏ	ĭ	ĕ	ă
must	soft	lost	mask	just
raft	fist	fast	list	rest
cast	tusk	desk	cost	gift
lift	brisk	best	task	dust
	loft	husk	left	nest

Short Vowel Words With Final Blends

ŏ u					

ŏ o					

ĭ i					

ĕ e					

ă a					

Say each short vowel word. Print the word under the box that shows its short vowel sound.

just	mask	lost	soft	must	rest	list	fast
fist	raft	gift	cost	desk	tusk	cast	dust
task	best	brisk	lift	nest	left	husk	loft

a (	e (	i (	o (	u (

(76) Sort 43: Short Vowel Words With Final Blends

ŭ	ŏ	ĭ	ĕ	ă
kiss	boss	class	moth	rich
which	toss	with	much	math
bath	rush	miss	cloth	such
brush	grass	fresh	guess	pass

Sort 44: Short Vowel Words With Final Digraphs (77)

Short Vowel Words With Final Digraphs

ŭ					

ŏ					

ĭ					

ĕ					

ă					

Sort 44: Short Vowel Words With Final Digraphs ⟨79⟩

Draw a picture of something with the short vowel sounds of a, e, i, o, and u. Write the word below each picture.

ă

ĕ

ĭ

ŏ

ŭ

Sort 44: Short Vowel Words With Final Digraphs

-n, -m, ran	-g, -t, -p, rag	-ng, -nt, -mp, rang
rung	tramp	run
pan	clam	ban
clamp	win	bag
wig	tram	rug
wing	pat	rap
trap	clap	bang
pant	ramp	ram

-n, -m, ran	-g, -t, -p, rag	-ng, -nt, -mp, rang

Say each word. Print the word below the box that shows its ending sound.

rung	tramp	run	clam	ban	clamp
win	bag	wig	tram	wing	pat
rap	trap	clap	bang	ramp	ram

-n, -m	-g, -t, -p	-ng, -mp

-mp		-ng	
sung	camp	king	jump	rang
limp	lamp	rung	sing	bump
bring	ramp	pump	ring	sang
stump	hung	stamp	swing	wing
		plump	thing	lump

-mp

-ng

Draw two pictures of things that end with -ng and -mp. Write the word below each picture.

-ng	-mp

Sort 46: Words That End in -ng, -mp

-nt	-nd	-nk
went	sand	pink
send	wink	hunt
bunk	land	bank
pant	junk	wind
print	stink	plant
blend	spent	stand
drink	want	

-nt	-nd	-nk

Say each word. Print the word below the box that shows its ending sound.

went	pink	wink	land	bank	blend
sand	hunt	bunk	want	stand	stink
junk	send	pant	wind	print	plant

-nt

-nd

-nk

Sort 47: Words That End in -nt, -nd, -nk

Short o and or

sock	fork	oddball
fox	for	corn	fort
drop	rot	born	sort
your	torn	short	work
spot	sport	storm	trot
word	shop	pond	horn

oddball					

fork					

sock					

Say each word in the box. Print each word under the key word that has the same vowel sound.

fox	for	born	spot
sport	pond	sort	torn
shop	rot	drop	storm

sock

fork

Sort 48: Short o and or

Short a and ar

cat	star ⭐	oddball	crab
car	far	drag	bark
farm	rag	snap	card
crash	art	war	dark
trap	yard	flag	jar
shark	brag	grand	

oddball					

star ⭐

cat 🐱

Say each word in the box. Print each word under the key word that has the same vowel sound.

farm	bark	brag	car
snap	crash	jar	trap
card	crab	dark	drag

cat

star

that's	he is	was not
do not	here's	can not
didn't	does not	that is
who is	what is	don't
can't	he's	who's
doesn't	here is	did not
what's	wasn't	

isn't	is not

it's	it is

Sort 50: Contractions (103)

Say each contraction. Print each contraction under the word that is part of the contraction.

didn't	that's	don't	here's	can't
wasn't	who's	he's	doesn't	what's

is

not

Sort 50: Contractions

Think about the vowel sound you hear in the name of each picture. Write the word on the line below the picture.

1.	2.	3.
4.	5.	6.
7.	8.	9. ←
10.	11.	12.
13.	14.	15.

Spell Check 4: Mixed Vowel Word Families (105)

Write the picture names on the lines.

 SPELL CHECK 5

1.	2.	3.
4.	5.	6.
7.	8.	9.
10.	11.	12.
13.	14.	15.

(106) Spell Check 5: Short Vowel Words

Write the picture names on the lines.

1. _____ _____

2. _____ _____

3. _____ _____

4. _____ _____

5. _____ _____

6. _____ _____

7. _____ _____

8. _____ _____

9. _____ _____

10. _____ _____

11. _____ _____

12. _____ _____

Copyright © SAVVAS Learning Company LLC. All Rights Reserved.

Spell Check 6: Preconsonantal Nasals   107

Write the picture names on the lines.

1.

_____

- - - - - - - - - - - -

_____

2.

_____

- - - - - - - - - - - -

_____

3.

_____

- - - - - - - - - - - -

_____

4.

_____

- - - - - - - - - - - -

_____

5.

_____

- - - - - - - - - - - -

_____

6.

_____

- - - - - - - - - - - -

_____

7.

_____

- - - - - - - - - - - -

_____

8.

_____

- - - - - - - - - - - -

_____

9.

_____

- - - - - - - - - - - -

_____

10.

_____

- - - - - - - - - - - -

_____

11.

_____

- - - - - - - - - - - -

_____

12.

_____

- - - - - - - - - - - -

_____